MY FIRST LOOK AT PLANETS

SWIRLS OF COLOR MAKE JUPITER LOOK PRETTY

Jupiter

TERESA WIMMER

CREATIVE EDUCATION

Published by Creative Education

P.O. Box 227, Mankato, Minnesota 56002

Creative Education is an imprint of The Creative Company

Designed by Rita Marshall

Photographs by Getty Images (Hulton Archive), Photo Researchers (Julian Baum / Science Photo Library, Chris Bjornberg / Science Source, Lynette Cook / Science Photo Library, Library of Congress / Science Source, NASA / Science Source, Science Photo Library, Detlev Van Ravenswaay), Tom Stack & Associates (TSADO / NASA)

Copyright © 2008 Creative Education

Printed in the United States of America

Library of Congress Cataloging-in-Publication Data

Wimmer, Teresa, 1975– Jupiter / by Teresa Wimmer.

p. cm. — (My first look at planets)

Includes index.

ISBN-13: 978-1-58341-517-7

I. Jupiter (Planet)—Juvenile literature. I. Title.

QB661.W735 2007   523.45—dc22   2006018247

First edition 9 8 7 6 5 4 3 2 1

JUPITER

THE BIG ONE

When people look up at the night sky, they might see a bright ball. From Earth, it looks like a star. But the bright ball is not a star. It is the **planet** Jupiter.

Jupiter is part of the **solar system**. Besides Jupiter, there are seven other planets. All of the planets move in an **orbit** around the sun. Jupiter is the fifth planet from the sun.

JUPITER IS BIGGER THAN ANY OTHER PLANET

Jupiter is not like Earth. Earth is made of rock, but Jupiter is made of **gas**. Jupiter is very big. All of the other planets put together could fit inside it!

Clouds and Storms

Jupiter looks pretty up close. It is covered in clouds. Some of the clouds are red or yellow. Others are white, orange, or brown. The clouds are always moving. They make Jupiter look like a striped beach ball.

Like all planets, Jupiter
is always spinning. It is
very light, so it spins fast.

Beneath the clouds are strong winds and lightning. There is also an egg-shaped spot on Jupiter. People call it the "Great Red Spot." The spot is really a big storm. It has been going on for years and years.

Near the clouds, Jupiter is very cold. But deep inside Jupiter, the air is as warm as the inside of a house.

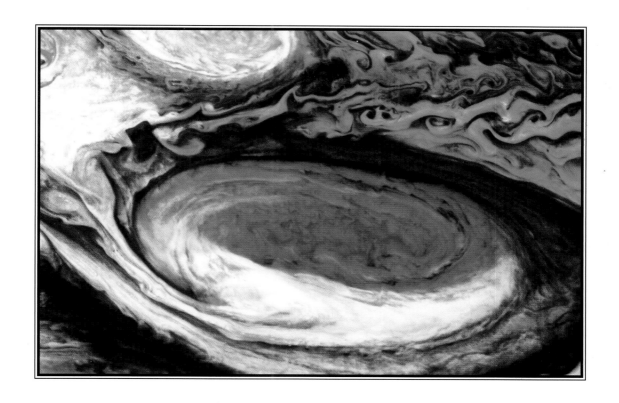

Besides the Great Red Spot,
Jupiter has many small stormy
spots. They look white.

Moons and Rings

Jupiter has at least 60 moons. They move in an orbit around Jupiter. Four of the moons are big. The rest are very small.

One of Jupiter's biggest moons is called Io (*EYE-oh*). Io has hot mountains called volcanoes. The volcanoes give off red, hot, melted rock called lava. They make Io look red and bumpy like a pizza.

At night, Jupiter's sky has lightning. There are bright lights called auroras (*uh-ROAR-uhs*), too.

EACH OF JUPITER'S MOONS LOOKS DIFFERENT

Jupiter has three rings around it. The rings look gray and thin. They are made mostly of dust. The dust is always moving. People think rocks crashed into some of Jupiter's moons a long time ago. Dust from the moons made the rings.

JUPITER'S RINGS MOVE IN A CIRCLE AROUND IT

Jupiter is far away from Earth. People cannot fly a spaceship to Jupiter and land on it. There is no ground for people to walk on. They would just sink into the gas.

But people send **probes** to Jupiter. The probes have special cameras. The cameras take pictures of Jupiter up close. Then the pictures are sent back to people on Earth.

One of Jupiter's moons is named Europa (*yoo-ROPE-uh*). It has strange volcanoes that throw out snowflakes!

IT TAKES PROBES SIX YEARS TO REACH JUPITER

JUPITER (LOWER LEFT) IS CALLED A "GAS GIANT"

The pictures do not show any people on Jupiter. They do not show any animals or plants, either. In a few years, people will send more probes to Jupiter. Then they will know more about the biggest planet!

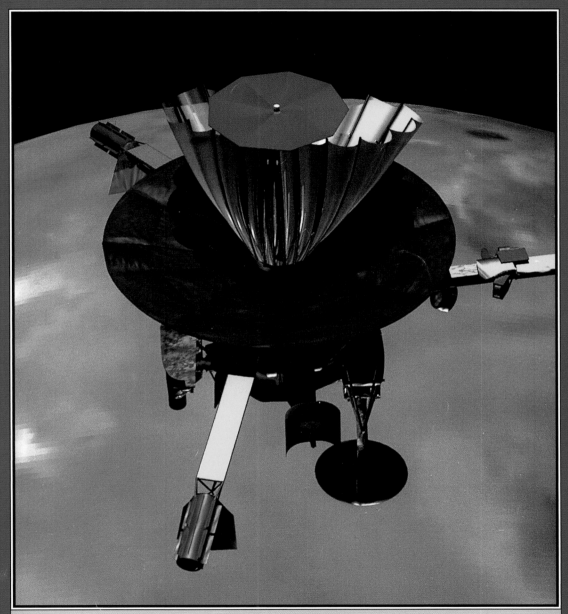

PROBES CAN TELL US A LOT ABOUT JUPITER

Hands-on: Make a Planet Jupiter

Jupiter is a big, bright planet. You can make your very own Jupiter!

What You Need

A big Styrofoam ball
A piece of yarn about eight
   inches (20 cm) long
Glue

Red, yellow, orange, and
   brown markers
Three gray pipe cleaners

What You Do

1. Color red, yellow, orange, and brown stripes on the Styrofoam ball. Leave a few white stripes between them. Color a red, egg-shaped spot near the middle.
2. Glue the gray pipe cleaners around the middle of the Styrofoam ball.
3. Glue one end of the yarn to the top of the ball.
4. Now you have your own planet Jupiter!

JUPITER MAY HAVE ROCK AT ITS CENTER

Index

Words to Know

gas—a kind of air; some gases are harmful to breathe

orbit—the path a planet takes around the sun or a moon takes around a planet

planet—a round object that moves around the sun

probes—special machines that fly around or land on a planet or a moon

solar system—the sun, the planets, and their moons

Read More

Rudy, Lisa Jo. *Planets!* New York: HarperCollins, 2005.

Taylor-Butler, Christine. *Jupiter*. New York: Scholastic, 2005.

Vogt, Gregory. *Solar System*. New York: Scholastic, 2001.

Explore the Web

Enchanted Learning: Jupiter http://www.zoomschool.com/subjects/astronomy/planets/jupiter

Funschool: Space http://funschool.kaboose.com/globe-rider/space/index.html?trnstl=1

StarChild: The Planet Jupiter http://starchild.gsfc.nasa.gov/docs/StarChild/solar_system_level1/jupiter.html